Father Hood

&

Faith

Rooted In Christ And Leading with Purpose

An Uplifting Devotional for
father's

Written by Daniel Okumbele

OnaHillPublishing.com

Published and Printed in the USA
First Printing Edition 2025.

Publisher: On a Hill Publishing co.

To every father striving to
love, lead, and live by faith—
This devotional is for you.

To the quiet warriors who wake early, pray hard,
work long, and show up even when it's hard—
your sacrifice is seen, and your legacy is being written
daily.

To the men becoming the fathers they never had, and
to those building on the faith of the fathers before
them— this journey matters.

May God strengthen your hands, soften your heart,
and guide every step you take.
You are not alone. You are called. And you are
equipped.

If you're holding this book, chances are you're doing your best to be the man your family needs. Let me just say—respect. Fatherhood isn't easy, but it matters more than most people will ever realize.

This devotional isn't about being a perfect dad. It's about showing up, walking with God, and letting Him shape you one day at a time. Some days you'll feel strong. Other days, you'll feel like you're barely holding it together. But every day, God is with you—and that changes everything.

These 30 days are here to challenge you, encourage you, and remind you that you're not alone. We're all figuring it out, and none of us get it right all the time. But our Father in Heaven is faithful, and He's building something eternal in and through you.

So take your time. Be real. Lean into grace.
And know this: you're not just raising kids—you're building a legacy.

Proud to walk this road with you,
Daniel Okumbele

How to Use This Devotional

Welcome to Fatherhood & Faith
This 30-day devotional is written to encourage, equip, and strengthen you as a father who desires to walk closely with God and lead your family with wisdom, love, and purpose.

What to Expect Each Day:

- Scripture – Begin with the verse for the day. Read it slowly. Let it guide your thoughts and set your heart on God.
- Devotional Reading – A brief reflection designed to help you apply biblical truth to your role as a father.
- Reflection Questions – These are meant to challenge and inspire deeper faith. Consider journaling your responses or discussing them with a trusted friend or mentor.
- Prayer – A focused, heartfelt prayer to help you draw near to God and commit each day to His guidance.

This devotional is organized around four weekly themes:

- Week 1: The Father's Identity in Christ
- Week 2: The Father as Leader and Servant
- Week 3: The Father's Role in the Family
- Week 4: The Father's Legacy of Faith

Each theme builds on the last, helping you grow in every area of your fatherhood and faith.

Tips for the Journey:

- Set a consistent time each day to connect with God— whether morning, midday, or evening.
- Be honest with yourself and with God. You don't need to have all the answers to draw near to Him.
- Go deeper by journaling, meditating on Scripture, or engaging in conversation with other dads.
- Allow grace. Progress, not perfection, is the goal.

Final Encouragement:

You are not alone. God has called and equipped you to lead your family in faith. This journey is not about performance— it's about presence, growth, and trust in the One who walks with you daily.

Let this devotional be a tool that points you to Christ and strengthens your role as a father who loves, leads, and lives by faith.

WEEK 1
The Father's Identity in Christ

Knowing who you are before leading your family

"See what great love the Father has lavished on us, that we should be called children of God! And that is what we are!"
— 1 John 3:1 (NIV)

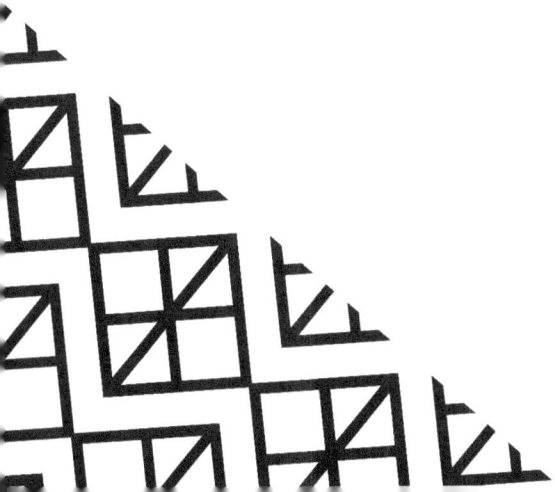

Day 1
You Are a Son First

Scripture:

"Because you are his sons, God sent the Spirit of his Son into our hearts, the Spirit who calls out, 'Abba, Father.' So you are no longer a slave, but God's child; and since you are his child, God has made you also an heir."
— Galatians 4:6–7 (NIV)

Devotion

Before you're a father, a husband, a provider, or a leader—you're a son. A son of the living God. This is your true identity, and it changes everything.

Many men carry the pressure of being strong, capable, and never failing. But God's Word reminds us that our foundation isn't in performance, but in relationship. You are not defined by your past, your paycheck, or your parenting mistakes. You are defined by the love of your heavenly Father.

Understanding your identity as a son brings freedom. It gives you permission to rest, to grow, and to lean on God instead of always trying to carry the weight alone. You are His—loved, known, and equipped. And as a son of God, you are never leading your family alone.

Reflect

- Do I truly trust God as my Father—or do I still live like I have to earn His approval?
- What would change in my relationship with God if I fully embraced my identity as His son?
- How can embracing my identity as His son strengthen my faith and leadership this week?

Prayer Moment

Abba (Father),

Thank You for calling me Your son. In a world that constantly tries to define me by my role, my performance, or my past, remind me that my true identity is found in You alone. Help me to rest in Your love instead of striving to earn it.

Teach me to live from a place of security, not insecurity—from faith, not fear. When I feel the pressure to have all the answers or carry the weight of my family alone, remind me that You are the ultimate Father, and I am never alone in this calling.

Let my relationship with You shape how I father my children—with grace, compassion, and courage. As I lead, help me be led by Your Spirit. Grow my faith as I grow in sonship. Let everything I do flow from the truth that I belong to You.

In Jesus' name,
Amen.

Day 2
Chosen and Called

Scripture:
"But you are a chosen people, a royal priesthood, a holy nation, God's special possession, that you may declare the praises of him who called you out of darkness into his wonderful light."
— 1 Peter 2:9 (NIV)

Devotion
Before your children were placed in your arms, God placed a calling on your life. You are not just "doing your best to figure it out"—you are chosen and called for a purpose far greater than yourself.

As a father, it's easy to feel unqualified. You may question your past, your abilities, or whether you have what it takes. But God doesn't call the perfect; He perfects those He calls. His calling is not based on your resume, but on His redemption.

You were chosen to lead your family in truth, love, and faith. You are a royal priest in your home—not to dominate, but to serve. Not to impress, but to represent the grace of a God who called you out of darkness into light.

Your calling is not just to raise children but to raise up sons and daughters of God. Walk confidently in that.

Reflect

- Am I living like a man God has called—or still doubting my place in His purpose?
- What fear or insecurity do I need to surrender so I can walk more confidently in God's calling over my life?

Prayer Moment

Lord,

Thank You for choosing me—not because I earned it, but because You love me. Even when I feel unqualified or overwhelmed, help me remember that Your calling on my life as a father is intentional and full of purpose.

Remind me that I am not alone or unequipped. You've placed Your Spirit in me. Strengthen me to walk boldly as the spiritual leader of my home. Let me represent Your love and truth well, and raise my children to know who they are in You.

Help me live not by fear, but by faith—faith in Your calling, faith in Your grace, and faith in Your presence in every moment of fatherhood. Use my life to declare Your goodness to my children and to the world.

In Jesus' name,
Amen.

Day 3
The Strength of Grace

Scripture:
"But he said to me, 'My grace is sufficient for you, for my power is made perfect in weakness.' Therefore I will boast all the more gladly about my weaknesses, so that Christ's power may rest on me."
— *2 Corinthians 12:9 (NIV)*

Devotion

As a father, you've likely had moments when you felt inadequate—when your patience ran out, your words missed the mark, or your strength gave way. The pressure to always be strong and dependable can feel heavy. But God never called you to be perfect—He called you to depend on His grace.

Grace doesn't excuse weakness; it empowers us through it. Paul reminds us that it's not in our flawless performance, but in our surrender, that Christ's power shows up. Fatherhood is a holy opportunity to lean into that truth daily.

When you mess up, grace restores. When you fall short, grace fills in. And when you feel weak, God's power stands tall. Your children don't need a perfect dad—they need a present, humble one who shows them what it looks like to rely on Jesus.

Let your weakness become the stage where God's grace shines the brightest.

Reflect

- When I face weakness, do I turn to God—or do I hide and try to handle it alone?
- How can I let God's grace transform not just my failures, but my everyday moments as a father?

Prayer Moment

Father God,

Thank You for reminding me that Your grace is not just a safety net, but a source of strength. I confess that there are days when I feel weak, frustrated, or unsure of what to do. But I also know that You are strong where I am not.

Teach me to lead with humility, not pressure—to model repentance, not perfection. Help me show my children that faith isn't about pretending to be strong, but about leaning on the One who is.

Let Your power rest on me. Fill my gaps with grace, and make me the kind of father whose life points to Your unshakable strength. I trust You in my weakness, because Your grace is more than enough.

In Jesus' name,
Amen.

Day 4
Walking in Newness

Scripture:

"We were therefore buried with him through baptism into death in order that, just as Christ was raised from the dead through the glory of the Father, we too may live a new life."
— Romans 6:4 (NIV)

Devotion

When you became a follower of Christ, your past lost its authority, and new life began. As a father, this truth changes the way you lead your home. You don't parent from your old self—you parent from the new life Jesus has given you.

Your children may not know every part of your past, but they will see how you live today. And today, you can choose to walk in newness—not chained to who you were, but empowered by who Christ is in you.

This new life is marked by grace, patience, forgiveness, and a growing faith. It doesn't mean you're perfect, but it means you're changed. And that transformation speaks louder than words—it shows your children what redemption really looks like.

God didn't just save you to get you to heaven. He saved you to reflect heaven in your home.

Reflect

- In what ways am I still allowing guilt or my past to define how I see myself as a father—and how can I surrender that to God today?
- What specific area of my life do I need to invite Jesus into more fully so I can walk in the freedom and newness He promises?
- How can I show my children that change is possible through faith in Jesus?

Prayer Moment

Jesus,

Thank You for giving me a new life—a life not defined by who I used to be, but by who I am in You. Sometimes I fall back into old habits or old thinking, but remind me daily that I am no longer that man. I've been raised with You, and I want to live like it.

Help me walk in newness with my children—not leading from shame, but from grace. Let my life be a testimony of transformation. Let my actions speak of Your power to change hearts, starting with mine.

Give me fresh strength today to lead with love, patience, and humility. May my faith not just be heard, but seen, in the way I live as a father.

In Your name,
Amen.

Day 5: Freedom from Performance

Scripture:

"It is for freedom that Christ has set us free. Stand firm, then, and do not let yourselves be burdened again by a yoke of slavery."
— Galatians 5:1 (NIV)

Devotion

So many fathers live under the silent pressure to perform—to always get it right, always have the answers, and never show weakness. But when you measure your worth by performance, you carry a weight you were never meant to bear.

God didn't call you to perform; He called you to be transformed.

In Christ, you are already loved. You are already accepted. You don't have to prove yourself to God—He proved His love for you on the cross. And the same grace that saved you is the grace that strengthens you as a father.

Freedom comes when you stop trying to earn what you've already received. God doesn't want your performance—He wants your presence. He wants your heart. Let go of the act, the mask, the silent pressure. Lead from rest. Parent from grace. And walk in the freedom Jesus paid for.

Reflect

- Am I striving to earn God's approval or resting in the truth that I already have it?
- What would it look like for me to lead my family from a place of freedom, not fear or pressure?

Prayer Moment

Father,

Thank You that I don't have to perform to be accepted by You. So often, I carry the burden of trying to be enough—for my kids, for my family, for myself. But Your Word reminds me that I am free because of Jesus.

Help me release the pressure to prove myself. Remind me that I am already loved, already chosen, already Yours. Teach me to lead from that truth and not from fear. Let my children see a father who walks in freedom, not perfection.

Draw me closer to You—not just in the moments when I feel strong, but especially when I feel weak. Thank You for giving me rest in Your grace and purpose in Your love.

In Jesus' name,
Amen.

Day 6
Faith Over Failure

Scripture:

"Though the righteous fall seven times, they rise again, but the wicked stumble when calamity strikes."
— Proverbs 24:16 (NIV)

Devotion

Every father will fail. Not once, not twice—but often. You'll lose your temper, make the wrong call, or miss a moment you wish you could get back. But failure doesn't disqualify you from being a good father. What matters is what you do next.

Scripture reminds us that the righteous aren't those who never fall, but those who get up again—anchored not in pride, but in faith. The difference between regret and redemption is turning toward God when you fall instead of away from Him.

Your children don't need a flawless father. They need a father who owns his mistakes and models what real faith looks like in failure: repentance, humility, and perseverance.

Every time you rise again, you're teaching them how to live with resilience and grace. Don't let failure speak louder than your faith. Let it drive you deeper into God's mercy—and back onto your feet.

Reflect

- How do I typically respond when I fail—by hiding in shame or rising in faith?
- What step of faith can I take today to show my children that God's grace is bigger than my mistakes?

Prayer Moment

God,

You know my flaws, my failures, and the places where I've fallen short as a father. Yet You still call me righteous—not because I'm perfect, but because I trust in You.

When I fall, remind me to rise—not in my own strength, but in Yours. Help me model repentance and resilience for my children. Let them see that failure doesn't define us—faith does.

Thank You for Your endless grace and for never giving up on me. Teach me to grow through my mistakes and to lead with humility and hope. Let my life be a testimony of Your redemptive power, even in broken places.

In Jesus' name,
Amen.

Day 7
Daily Surrender

Scripture:
"Trust in the Lord with all your heart and lean not on your own understanding; in all your ways submit to him, and he will make your paths straight."
— Proverbs 3:5–6 (NIV)

Devotion

Fatherhood doesn't come with a manual—but it does come with a God who walks with you every step of the way.

You won't always know what to do. There will be days when the decisions are heavy, when the path seems unclear, or when you feel the weight of leading others while feeling unsure yourself. That's where daily surrender becomes essential.

Trusting God is not a one-time decision—it's a daily practice. Submitting your heart, your plans, your parenting, your fears—again and again. When you stop leaning on your own understanding and begin to rely on God, He leads you with wisdom, peace, and clarity.

Surrender is not weakness—it's strength in its most powerful form. It's a father saying, "I can't do this alone, and I don't have to." Let that be your anchor. Let trust be your legacy.

Reflect
- What part of my role as a father have I been trying to control instead of surrendering to God?
- How can I build a daily rhythm of trust and submission to strengthen my walk with

Prayer Moment
Lord,
Today, I surrender again. I give You my worries, my questions, my efforts, and my role as a father. I don't have all the answers, but You do. Teach me to trust You more deeply—not just in the big moments, but in the quiet, daily ones.

Help me let go of control and lean fully on Your wisdom. Shape my heart, direct my steps, and guide my decisions. Let my children see in me a man who is led by Your Spirit, who seeks You first, and who walks by faith.

Thank You that I don't have to figure it all out alone. I trust You with my family, my future, and my fatherhood.

In Jesus' name,
Amen.

*W*eekly Check-in

What are three things I'm grateful for this week?

1. ....

2. ....

3. ....

What am I praying for this week?

....

....

....

....

....

How did I reflect God's Love this week?

....

....

....

....

....

What areas of my life do I need to improve / surrender to Christ so that I may be more like Him?

....

....

....

....

"You can't pour from an empty cup—take care of yourself first."

WEEK 2
The Father as Leader and Servant
leading with love, humility, and conviction.

"Now that I, your Lord and Teacher, have washed your feet, you also should wash one another's feet. I have set you an example that you should do as I have done for you."
  -John 13:14–15 (NIV)

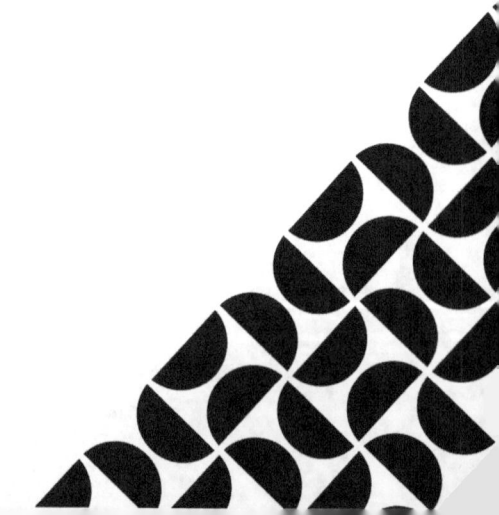

Day 8
Leading by Example

Scripture:

"Don't let anyone look down on you because you are young, but set an example for the believers in speech, in conduct, in love, in faith and in purity."
— 1 Timothy 4:12 (NIV)

Devotion

Leadership in the home isn't just about what you say—it's about how you live. As a father, your children are watching your every move. They learn what faith looks like not just from your words, but from your daily choices.

Paul's instruction to Timothy wasn't just for young pastors—it's a challenge to all believers, especially fathers. Set an example in your speech. Let your words bring life and truth. In your conduct, show integrity and self-control. In love, demonstrate patience and sacrifice. In faith, walk with trust in God. And in purity, live with integrity in a world that often lacks it.

You won't do it perfectly, but consistency matters more than perfection. Your example has more influence than you realize. Whether you're aware of it or not, you're shaping the way your children will view God, relationships, and leadership.

You don't need a title to lead—you need conviction, humility, and a heart fully surrendered to Christ.

Reflect

- What kind of example am I setting for my children in how I speak, act, and express my faith?
- What specific area of my life do I need to surrender to God so my leadership reflects Christ more clearly?

Prayer Moment

Father,

Thank You for the opportunity to lead my family—not through force, but by example. Help me live in a way that points my children to You. Let my words be filled with grace and truth. Let my actions reflect honor and wisdom.

Lord, I know I won't always get it right, but give me the strength to stay consistent and the humility to admit when I fall short. May my children see in me a man who genuinely follows Christ, not just on Sunday but every day.

Make my life a living testimony of Your grace and love. Teach me to lead with authenticity, passion, and purity—so my example becomes a light that guides them toward You.

In Jesus' name,
Amen.

Day 9
Servant Leadership

Scripture:

"For even the Son of Man did not come to be served, but to serve, and to give his life as a ransom for many."
— Mark 10:45 (NIV)

Devotion

The world defines leadership as control, status, and power—but Jesus redefined it as service, sacrifice, and love. As a father, your greatest influence doesn't come from authority—it comes from how you serve.

Jesus had every right to be worshiped and waited on, yet He knelt to wash feet. He didn't demand loyalty—He demonstrated love. True leadership begins when you place others before yourself, especially in your home.

It means choosing patience over anger. Listening before reacting. Leading your family spiritually, even when it's not convenient. Serving when you're tired. Loving when it's hard.

Being a servant leader doesn't make you weak—it makes you Christlike. Your kids may not always understand the sacrifices you make, but they will remember the way you laid your life down for them, one small act of love at a time.

When you lead by serving, you reflect the very heart of Jesus.

Reflect

- In what ways can I serve my family today that reflect the humility of Christ?
- Do I view leadership as an opportunity to serve—or as a burden to carry?

Prayer Moment

Jesus,
You could have ruled from a throne, but You chose a towel and basin.
Teach me to lead like You—with humility, compassion, and a heart to serve.

In the pressures of life and leadership, help me not to seek recognition but to seek Your heart. Give me strength when I feel unseen, grace when I feel stretched, and joy in the quiet acts of love that shape my family.

Let my children learn what greatness looks like—not through my status, but through my sacrifice. May the way I serve them speak louder than any words I say. Help me become a father who leads by going low—because that's where Your presence dwells.

In Your name,
Amen.

Day 10
Courage to Lead

Scripture:
"Have I not commanded you? Be strong and courageous. Do not be afraid; do not be discouraged, for the Lord your God will be with you wherever you go."
— Joshua 1:9 (NIV)

Devotion

Leadership as a father can be daunting. You're expected to guide, protect, provide, and model faith. But what happens when you feel inadequate or overwhelmed? That's where courage comes in—not the absence of fear, but the decision to move forward despite it.

Joshua stood on the edge of the unknown, called to lead a people into a promise that came with battles. God didn't promise him an easy path—He promised His presence. And that made all the difference.

You won't have every answer. You'll face difficult decisions, moments of doubt, and even failure. But God isn't asking you to be perfect—He's asking you to be faithful. And faithfulness requires courage.

Courage to love when it's not returned. To stand firm when it's unpopular. To admit when you're wrong. To follow Christ when the world pulls in the opposite direction.

God is with you—not just in church, but in the living room, at the dinner table, in the quiet moments of fatherhood. You don't lead alone. He goes before you.

Reflect

- What fears or doubts are holding me back from leading with full confidence in God?
- How can I intentionally lean into God's presence and promises as I lead my family?

Prayer Moment

Father,

Thank You that I don't have to face this calling alone. So often I feel the weight of fatherhood—the decisions, the expectations, the pressure. But You remind me to be strong and courageous, not because I'm capable, but because You are with me.

Strengthen my heart today. Fill me with holy confidence—not in myself, but in You. Help me to lead boldly, speak truthfully, and love fearlessly. When I feel uncertain, remind me of Your promises. When I feel weak, remind me of Your power.

Let my courage be contagious in my home. May my children see a father who walks by faith, not fear.

In Jesus' name,
Amen.

Day 11
Shepherding the Heart

Scripture:
"Above all else, guard your heart, for everything you do flows from it."
— Proverbs 4:23 (NIV)

Devotion

It's easy to focus on behavior as a father—correcting wrongs, setting rules, rewarding obedience. But true leadership reaches deeper than outward actions—it shepherds the heart.

Proverbs reminds us that the heart is the wellspring of life. What flows out —words, attitudes, habits—starts from within. That's why your children don't just need discipline; they need discipleship. They need a father who not only guards his own heart but also tends to theirs with intentional love and care.

Shepherding the heart means taking time to listen, not just instruct. It means asking what's going on beneath the behavior. It means speaking identity and truth when the world tries to shape their worth.

But before you can shepherd your child's heart, you must first invite God to shape yours. A heart anchored in Christ is steady, compassionate, and discerning. When your heart is full of His wisdom and grace, you're equipped to lead your children's hearts toward Him.

Reflect
- Am I more focused on correcting my child's behavior or guiding their heart toward God?
- What condition is my own heart in, and how is it affecting the way I lead and parent?

Prayer Moment
Father,
Teach me to be a shepherd of hearts, not just a manager of behavior. Help me see beyond actions to what's happening in the hearts of my children. Give me Your discernment to speak life into them, to guide them with truth, and to lead them in love.

Lord, guard my heart as well. Let everything I do as a father flow from a place of grace, humility, and trust in You. When I'm impatient, slow me down. When I'm distracted, refocus me. Make my heart more like Yours so that my leadership reflects Your character.

Help me to be present, engaged, and intentional as I raise the sons and daughters You've entrusted to me.

In Jesus' name,
Amen.

MY NOTES & PRAYERS

Day 12
Consistency Over Perfection

Scripture:
"The righteous lead blameless lives; blessed are their children after them."
— Proverbs 20:7 (NIV)

Devotion
Perfection can be paralyzing—but consistency is powerful. As a father, you'll have moments of failure. You'll lose your temper. You'll forget something important. You'll say the wrong thing. But what will stand out to your children in the long run isn't whether you were perfect—it's whether you were faithful.

Consistency means showing up again and again. It means repenting when you fall and getting back up with God's help. It means choosing to live with integrity, even when no one is watching. The small, steady choices you make each day become the building blocks of trust, character, and legacy.

God isn't asking you to impress your children—He's calling you to model what a life of grace and faith looks like. When they see you pursue God through both victories and mistakes, they'll learn that following Christ isn't about being flawless—it's about being faithful.

Reflect

- Where is God calling me to be more consistent in my leadership at home?
- How can I show my children the power of steady, faithful obedience today?
- Do I believe God can use my imperfect efforts to leave a lasting impact on my children?

Prayer Moment

Father,

Thank You that I don't have to be perfect to be a good dad.

You've never asked that of me. You've only called me to walk with You daily—to keep showing up, to keep trusting, and to keep leaning on Your strength.

Help me to be consistent in my love, my words, my presence, and my walk with You. When I fail, remind me of Your grace. When I succeed, keep me humble. May my children see not a perfect father, but one who faithfully follows a perfect Savior.

Shape my legacy through faithfulness. Help me lead in a way that draws my family closer to You.

In Jesus' name,
Amen.

Day 13
Standing Firm in Faith

Scripture:
"Be on your guard; stand firm in the faith; be courageous; be strong."
— *1 Corinthians 16:13 (NIV)*

Devotion
A father's faith sets the tone for his home. In a world full of shifting values, loud opinions, and constant distractions, your ability to stand firm in faith is one of the greatest gifts you can give your family.

Paul's words to the Corinthian church are bold and timely: be on guard, stand firm, be courageous, be strong. This isn't a passive kind of faith. It's active, intentional, and deeply rooted in truth. As a father, this means guarding your heart, protecting your home, and anchoring your decisions in God's Word—even when it's not popular or convenient.

Standing firm doesn't mean being rigid—it means being rooted. It means holding your ground in prayer when fear creeps in. It means choosing integrity when compromise feels easier. It means clinging to God's promises when circumstances look uncertain.

Your children need to see a man who doesn't just talk about faith, but lives it boldly. When storms come, they'll remember how you stood—on your knees in prayer, with your eyes on Jesus.

Reflect

- Where in my life do I need to take a stronger stand for my faith and convictions?
- What example of spiritual strength do I want to leave for my children to follow?

Prayer Moment

Lord God,

Strengthen my faith so I can lead with courage and conviction. When the pressures of life press in, remind me that You are my solid foundation. Help me to be vigilant—not fearful, but aware. Keep me anchored in truth and unwavering in my devotion to You.

Teach me to be a protector and a priest in my home. May my children see me clinging to You in both the victories and the valleys. Let my faith be the lighthouse they look toward when the waves rise.

Give me strength that doesn't come from myself, but from the power of Your Spirit. Help me to lead by standing—firm, faithful, and full of grace.

In Jesus' name,
Amen.

MY NOTES & PRAYERS

Day 14
Leading Through Prayer

Scripture:

"Do not be anxious about anything, but in every situation, by prayer and petition, with thanksgiving, present your requests to God. And the peace of God, which transcends all understanding, will guard your hearts and your minds in Christ Jesus."
— Philippians 4:6–7 (NIV)

Devotion

A father's strength doesn't come from having all the answers—it comes from knowing where to take the questions. Prayer is your most powerful tool as a leader. It's where battles are won, peace is found, and wisdom is received.

When you lead through prayer, you show your children that strength is not about control, but surrender. They need to see you go to God when you're worried, when you're thankful, and when you don't know what to do. It teaches them that real men seek God not just in crisis, but in the quiet, everyday moments.

Prayer isn't just for your own peace—it's how you fight for your family. It's how you cover your children when you can't be with them. It's how you release your fears and receive God's strength.

Leading through prayer is leading with humility and power.

It acknowledges that you're not the ultimate protector, provider, or planner —God is. And that is the safest, strongest place to lead from.

Reflect
- Is prayer my first response or my last resort when challenges arise in fatherhood?
- How can I model a life of consistent prayer to my children this week?

Prayer Moment
Heavenly Father,

Thank You for the gift of prayer—that I can come to You anytime, with everything. Teach me to lead my home from a posture of prayer. Not as a last resort, but as a first response.

Help me to bring You my worries instead of carrying them alone. Help me to be an example of what it means to trust You fully. May my children see me on my knees, seeking You in every decision, every joy, every burden.

God, give me Your peace when my heart feels heavy. Let my prayers plant seeds of faith in my family that will grow for generations. Let my leadership be marked not by pride or control, but by constant communion with You.

In Jesus' name,
Amen.

Weekly Check-in

What are three things I'm grateful for this week?

1.
....

2.
....

3.
....

What am I praying for this week?

....

....

....

....

....

How did I reflect God's Love this week?

....

....

....

....

What areas of my life do I need to improve / surrender to Christ so that I may be more like Him?

....

....

....

....

"You can't pour from an empty cup—take care of yourself first."

WEEK 3
The Father's Role in the Family

Building godly relationships with your spouse and children

"But as for me and my household, we will serve the Lord."
  -Joshua 24:15 (NIV)

Day 15
Loving Like Christ

Scripture:
"Husbands, love your wives, just as Christ loved the church and gave himself up for her."
— Ephesians 5:25 (NIV)

Devotion

The way you love your wife sets the spiritual tone for your entire household. Paul's instruction is clear—and challenging. Love your wife the way Christ loves the church: sacrificially, faithfully, unconditionally.

This is not about perfection but about pursuing a posture of selflessness. Christ gave up His own comfort, rights, and even His life for the church. As a father and husband, you're called to mirror that kind of love—a love that puts your spouse's needs before your own, that forgives quickly, serves joyfully, and speaks life constantly.

When your children see you loving their mother this way, they learn what respect, honor, and commitment look like. You're not just modeling marriage—you're modeling the Gospel.

Whether you're in a season of strength or struggle in your relationship, remember: your love can be a daily reflection of Christ. It's not about how strong you are—it's about how surrendered you are.

Reflect

- How can I love my wife more sacrificially this week—through my words, time, or actions?
- What areas of my marriage need to be surrendered more fully to Christ's example of love?

Prayer Moment

Father,

Thank You for the gift of my wife and for the calling to love her as Christ loves the church. I confess that I often fall short of this standard, but I ask for Your grace and strength to lead in love.

Help me to be a servant-leader in my home—to listen well, to speak kindly, to support her in every season. Teach me to lay down pride, selfishness, and frustration, and to choose love even when it's hard.

Let my love for my wife be a witness to my children and to the world. Shape my heart to look more like Yours so that my marriage can reflect Your glory.

In Jesus' name,
Amen.

Day 16
The Power of Words

Scripture:
"The tongue has the power of life and death, and those who love it will eat its fruit."
— Proverbs 18:21 (NIV)

Devotion
Your words as a father carry immense weight. With them, you can build your family up—or tear them down. Scripture reminds us that the tongue holds the power of life and death. That means your words can either speak life into your spouse and children or slowly drain their spirit.

It's easy to overlook a sarcastic comment or an impatient tone. But what you say—and how you say it—leaves a lasting impression. Your children are listening, learning, and internalizing your words. Are they hearing encouragement, blessing, truth, and grace? Or criticism, anger, and discouragement?

And when it comes to your wife, your words should be a covering—offering strength, support, and honor. Speak life into her identity. Affirm her worth. Be the voice that reminds her of who she is in Christ.

Words spoken in love create an atmosphere where faith can grow and relationships can thrive.

So choose your words like seeds. Because what you sow, you and your family will one day reap.

Reflect

- Are my daily words in the home building up my family or breaking them down?
- What is one intentional way I can use my words this week to speak life into my wife or children?

Prayer Moment

Lord,

Help me to use my words wisely. Forgive me for the times I've spoken in frustration or carelessness. Teach me to speak life into my home—to encourage rather than criticize, to bless rather than belittle.

Let my tongue be a tool for healing and hope. Help me to honor my wife and uplift my children with my words. May everything that comes from my mouth reflect Your truth and Your love.

Remind me that my voice matters in my home—and that when I speak with faith, kindness, and love, I create space for Your presence to move.

In Jesus' name,
Amen.

Day 17
Correcting with Compassion

Scripture:

"No discipline seems pleasant at the time, but painful. Later on, however, it produces a harvest of righteousness and peace for those who have been trained by it."
— Hebrews 12:11 (NIV)

Devotion

Discipline is one of the most sacred responsibilities of a father—and one of the most challenging. It's easy to correct out of frustration or to demand obedience without explanation. But God calls us to a higher standard: discipline that is rooted in love and guided by compassion.

Just as our Heavenly Father disciplines us for our good, you're called to correct your children not to control them, but to shape their character. Discipline should not break their spirit, but strengthen it. It's not just about consequences; it's about training them in the way they should go.

Correcting with compassion means taking time to explain the why behind the what. It means listening before you correct and guiding them back to truth with patience, not punishment. Your children need to know that even when they fail, they are still loved—and that discipline is not rejection but redirection.

When you lead correction with the heart of the Father, you help cultivate a home of peace, grace, and godly growth.

Reflect
- When I discipline my children, do I reflect the heart of God—or my own frustration?
- How can I create a culture of correction that builds trust, truth, and grace in my home?

Prayer Moment
Father,
Thank You for Your loving discipline in my life. You correct me not to shame me, but to shape me—and I want to reflect that same heart in my parenting.

Help me not to discipline out of anger, but out of love. Give me wisdom to correct with clarity and compassion. Help me teach my children the difference between guilt and growth—between making a mistake and being shaped by it.

Give me patience when I feel stretched, and help me reflect Your mercy even in moments of correction. May every lesson point them back to You.

In Jesus' name,
Amen.

Day 18
The Gift of Time

Scripture:
"There is a time for everything, and a season for every activity under the heavens."
— Ecclesiastes 3:1 (NIV)

Devotion

Time is one of the most valuable gifts you can give your family—and one of the easiest to overlook. With the demands of work, responsibilities, and even ministry, it's tempting to assume that providing for your family is the same as being present with them. But your children and your spouse don't just need what you bring home—they need you.

Ecclesiastes reminds us that everything has its season, and there is a time for every activity. That means you'll never regret slowing down to sit with your child, to go on that walk, or to look your spouse in the eye and ask how she's doing. These seemingly small moments become lasting memories—and deep investments into your family's spiritual and emotional well-being.

Time is also a mirror of your values. What you give your time to reveals what truly matters to you. Let your calendar reflect your commitment not only to lead your family, but to love them with intentional time and undivided attention.

In a world that pulls you in every direction, be the father who stays present in the moment. Because presence speaks louder than any words ever could.

Reflect

- Does the way I spend my time reflect the priorities God has given me as a husband and father?
- What simple, intentional moment can I create this week to connect deeply with my spouse or children?

Prayer Moment

Lord,

Thank You for the gift of time. Help me not to take it for granted. In the rush of daily life, teach me to slow down, to be fully present with my family, and to see the moments You've given me as opportunities to love well.

Show me what to say no to, so I can say yes to what truly matters. Help me to treasure the little things—bedtime conversations, shared meals, quiet moments—and to realize these are where connection is built.

Let my time reflect my love, and let my presence bring peace and stability to my home.

In Jesus' name,
Amen.

Day 19
Being Present

Scripture:

"These commandments that I give you today are to be on your hearts. Impress them on your children. Talk about them when you sit at home and when you walk along the road, when you lie down and when you get up."
— Deuteronomy 6:6–7 (NIV)

Devotion

Being present is more than just being physically near—it's about being emotionally and spiritually engaged. Deuteronomy 6 calls fathers to teach and lead their children in everyday moments—when sitting at home, walking, lying down, and rising up. That's not a command for a one-time event. It's a call to a lifestyle of faithful presence.

Your presence offers your children stability, safety, and a living example of what it looks like to follow God daily. Whether it's a shared meal, bedtime prayer, or a spontaneous conversation in the car, these ordinary moments become sacred opportunities to point them to Christ.

In a world filled with distractions, it takes intentional effort to stay engaged. Phones, stress, and busyness can pull your attention away. But your presence speaks volumes—sometimes more than any lecture or rule. It shows your children they matter and that your relationship with them is a priority.

And most importantly, being present allows your children to see your faith in action. They won't just hear about God—they'll watch how you trust Him.

Reflect
- Am I fully present when I'm with my family, or are distractions taking priority over meaningful connection?
- How can I intentionally turn everyday moments into opportunities to share my faith with my children?

Prayer Moment
Father,
Thank You for entrusting me with the hearts of my children. Teach me how to be truly present—not just in body, but in spirit. Help me to slow down, to listen well, and to see the daily moments as divine opportunities to lead them in faith.

Keep me from being distracted or distant. Instead, stir in me a desire to engage—to know their thoughts, guide their hearts, and walk with them in grace and truth. Let my presence reflect Your love, and may my life draw them closer to You.

In Jesus' name,
Amen.

Day 20
Generational Blessing

Scripture:
"Blessed is the man who fears the Lord, who finds great delight in his commands. His children will be mighty in the land; the generation of the upright will be blessed."
— Psalm 112:1–2 (NIV)

Devotion

As a father, you are building more than a home—you are building a legacy. Psalm 112 reminds us that the man who fears the Lord leaves a blessing that outlives him. His children, and even generations to come, reap the fruit of his faithfulness.

This kind of generational blessing doesn't come from wealth, status, or perfection. It comes from obedience, reverence, and a life shaped by God's Word. When your children see you honor God—not just on Sundays but in your everyday choices—they are being planted in soil that produces spiritual strength for years to come.

Every time you pray with your family, resist temptation, forgive quickly, or lead with integrity, you are sowing seeds of blessing into your lineage. These are the moments that shape how your children view God—and eventually, how they lead their own families.

You may not see all the fruit now, but your faithfulness is writing a story far greater than your own. You are a bridge to blessing—building a legacy that points to Jesus.

Reflect
- What kind of spiritual legacy am I building for my children and grandchildren?
- What habits or values do I need to strengthen to ensure I'm sowing seeds of blessing into future generations?

Prayer Moment
Lord,
Thank You for the incredible responsibility and privilege of fatherhood. Help me to live with the kind of reverence and obedience that brings blessing not only to my life, but to the generations that follow me.

Teach me to lead my family with faith, to model consistency in Your Word, and to create a spiritual foundation that my children can stand on. Even when I don't see results right away, give me the courage to sow faithfully—trusting that You will bring the increase.

May my life tell a story of Your grace that echoes in my family for generations.

In Jesus' name,
Amen.

Day 21
Honoring the Role of Mother

Scripture:
"Her children arise and call her blessed; her husband also, and he praises her: 'Many women do noble things, but you surpass them all.'"
— Proverbs 31:28–29 (NIV)

Devotion

Fatherhood doesn't exist in a vacuum. For many, it operates alongside the vital presence of a mother—whether in marriage, co-parenting, or in partnership through life's challenges. As fathers, one of the most powerful things we can do for our children is honor and affirm their mother.

Proverbs 31 praises a woman of noble character, and it paints a picture of a home where her worth is recognized and her contributions are celebrated. When a father speaks well of his children's mother—especially in front of them—he plants seeds of respect, unity, and security in their hearts.

Honoring the mother of your children doesn't mean she's perfect. It means you lead by grace. You praise what's praiseworthy, support her dignity in times of disagreement, and show your children how love works—even when it's not easy. It means backing her up in discipline, appreciating her sacrifices, and protecting her heart from criticism—even in private.

If you are married, this means lifting her up with your words and actions. If you're co-parenting, it means refusing to let bitterness or pride poison your children's view of their mom. If you're parenting after loss, it means helping your children cherish her memory.

When a wife feels secure, seen, and supported, it creates a foundation of peace and strength that blesses the entire home.

A father who honors the mother honors God's design for the family.

Reflect

- Do my words and actions consistently honor my wife in front of our children?
- How can I better support and uplift the role of mother in our family this week?

Prayer Moment

Father,

Thank You for the gift of my wife and for the vital role she plays in our family. Help me to honor her with my words, my actions, and my heart. Teach me to see her as You do—strong, beautiful, and deeply loved.

Forgive me for any times I've been dismissive or critical. Instead, let my voice be one of encouragement and praise. Help me to model respect and unity in front of our children, so they learn to value and honor the incredible role of motherhood.

Use me to bless her, protect her, and point her back to You. May our partnership reflect Your love to our home and to the world.

In Jesus' name,
Amen.

Weekly Check-in

What are three things I'm grateful for this week?

1.
....

2.
....

3.
....

What am I praying for this week?

....

....

....

....

....

How did I reflect God's Love this week?

....

....

....

....

....

What areas of my life do I need to improve / surrender to Christ so that I may be more like Him?

....

....

....

....

....

"You can't pour from an empty cup—take care of yourself first."

WEEK 4
The Father's Legacy of Faith

Living and leaving a lasting example of faith

"But the mercy of the Lord is from everlasting to everlasting on those who fear Him, and His righteousness to children's children."
— *Psalm 103:17 (NKJV)*

Day 22
Faith That Speaks

Scripture:

"Fix these words of mine in your hearts and minds; tie them as symbols on your hands and bind them on your foreheads. Teach them to your children, talking about them when you sit at home and when you walk along the road, when you lie down and when you get up."
— Deuteronomy 11:18–19 (NIV)

Devotion

A father's legacy of faith begins with a heart and mind anchored in God's Word—but it doesn't stop there. The legacy becomes lasting when that faith is spoken—regularly, intentionally, and sincerely. Moses charged the people of Israel to keep God's Word close and to talk about it often, especially with their children.

As a father, your voice carries weight. Your words have the power to build up, to instruct, to bless, and to guide. And when those words are filled with God's truth, they shape how your children understand life and faith.

Your faith doesn't have to be polished or perfect. It simply needs to be present—spoken in everyday moments: during a car ride, at the dinner table, or while praying at bedtime. When your children hear you speak about God, they begin to see that faith isn't just a Sunday ritual—it's a daily relationship.

Let your words reflect the Word. Let your life be a living testimony. And let your faith speak—loud enough that your children carry its echo for generations.

Reflect

- When was the last time I had a meaningful conversation with my children about God, Scripture, or faith?
- What intentional habits can I develop to make spiritual conversations a regular part of our family's life?

Prayer Moment

FLord,
Let my faith be more than private thoughts or good intentions. Help me to speak of You with confidence, joy, and consistency. Let my words carry Your wisdom and truth into the hearts of my children.

Give me the boldness to talk about You in everyday life—not just in formal devotion, but in natural, meaningful moments. May my home be filled with reminders of Your love, and may my children grow up knowing that You were at the center of our family.

Let my voice echo Your Word—today and for generations to come.
In Jesus' name,
Amen.

Day 23
A Man of Integrity

Scripture:

"Lord, who may dwell in your sacred tent? Who may live on your holy mountain? The one whose walk is blameless, who does what is righteous, who speaks the truth from their heart."
— Psalm 15:1–2 (NIV)

Devotion

In a world where integrity is often optional, God calls fathers to a higher standard. Psalm 15 paints a portrait of the kind of man who lives close to God—a man who is honest, righteous, and consistent in character. This kind of man doesn't just say the right things; he lives them.

As a father, your integrity leaves an imprint deeper than you may realize. Children may forget lectures, but they remember how you handled pressure, how you treated others when no one was looking, and how you honored your word. Integrity isn't about being perfect—it's about being real, being faithful, and choosing what's right even when it's costly or inconvenient.

When your life is aligned with God's truth, your legacy becomes a foundation your children can stand on. You give them a front-row seat to faith in action. And in doing so, you teach them not just how to believe—but how to live with courage, consistency, and conviction.

Reflect

- What area of my life is God calling me to walk in greater integrity?
- How can my example help my children see the value of truth, even when it's hard?

Prayer Moment

Father,

Shape me into a man of integrity—someone who reflects Your character in every area of life. Help me to walk in righteousness, speak with truth, and act with humility even when no one else sees. Let my private life honor You just as much as my public one.

Forgive me for any moments I've compromised. Restore my heart and give me the strength to lead with honesty and grace. May my life be a testimony that points my children not to perfection, but to the power of a faithful and forgiving God.

I want my legacy to be one of truth, love, and unwavering trust in You.
In Jesus' name,
Amen.

Day 24
Teaching by Living

Scripture:

"Similarly, encourage the young men to be self-controlled. In everything set them an example by doing what is good. In your teaching show integrity, seriousness and soundness of speech that cannot be condemned."
— Titus 2:6–7 (NIV)

Devotion

Fathers are teachers—not always by words, but always by example. The apostle Paul's instruction to Titus reminds us that the most effective lessons are those lived out. Children may hear what we say, but they believe what they see.

Whether you realize it or not, your daily choices—how you treat others, handle stress, manage money, or respond to difficulty—are teaching your children what it means to follow Christ. Your actions preach louder than any sermon. When you model self-control, kindness, humility, and truth, you're not just building your own life; you're building theirs.

No father is perfect, but consistency in living out your faith builds trust. Even your repentance becomes a lesson—showing them that grace is real, and growth is always possible. Let your life be the curriculum and your heart the teacher. Lead them not just to know about God, but to see Him alive in you.

Reflect

- What message is my daily life sending to my children about who God is?
- How can I be more intentional about teaching my children through my actions this week?

Prayer Moment

God,

Thank You for entrusting me with the responsibility of shaping lives. I know that my actions speak louder than my words, so help me live in a way that points my children to You. Let my example be one of love, discipline, humility, and wisdom.

When I fall short, give me the courage to confess, and the grace to grow. Help me lead with authenticity so that my children see a real, active faith— one that clings to You through every season. May my life teach them how to walk with You daily.

In Jesus' name,
Amen.

Day 25
Building on the Rock

Scripture:

"Therefore everyone who hears these words of mine and puts them into practice is like a wise man who built his house on the rock. The rain came down, the streams rose, and the winds blew and beat against that house; yet it did not fall, because it had its foundation on the rock."
— Matthew 7:24–25 (NIV)

Devotion

Every father is a builder—not just of homes or careers, but of legacies. Jesus' parable reminds us that the difference between a house that stands and one that collapses is not the presence of storms, but the strength of the foundation.

As a father, your decisions, priorities, and values lay the groundwork for the lives of those who follow you. When your life is built on the solid foundation of God's Word—when you not only hear but also apply it—you are building a spiritual shelter that can weather any storm.

There will be wind. There will be floods. But when your faith is real and active, your home becomes a place of peace and security—not because life is easy, but because your hope is anchored in something eternal.

You are not just building for yourself—you're building for your children and their future. Every act of obedience, every step of faith, every godly choice adds another stone to a lasting foundation.

Reflect

- Is my life built more on God's Word or on temporary things like success or comfort?
- What specific actions can I take to build a stronger spiritual foundation for my family?

Prayer Moment

Lord,

You are my Rock and my Refuge. Help me to build my life on Your truth, not just hearing Your Word but putting it into action. Strengthen my foundation so that I can stand firm for my family through every season.

When life gets overwhelming, help me trust that You are the one holding everything together. Teach me to lead by example, to build with wisdom, and to trust You in both the sunshine and the storm. May my life and my legacy be rooted in You.

In Jesus' name,
Amen.

Day 26
The Power of Prayer for Your Children

Scripture:
"The prayer of a righteous person is powerful and effective."
— James 5:16b (NIV)

Devotion
One of the greatest gifts you can give your children is not something you buy—it's the prayers you pray. Prayer is not a last resort; it is a powerful tool that shapes the spiritual atmosphere of your home and influences your children in ways words and actions never could.

Your prayers can go places your presence cannot. Long after your children have left your home, your prayers follow them. When you pray over their hearts, their choices, their future, and their faith, you are doing more than asking God to bless them—you're standing in the gap and partnering with Him in their journey.

You may not always have the perfect words as a father, but when you bring your children before God, He hears. He works in the quiet, behind the scenes, sometimes slowly—but always faithfully.

Your legacy as a praying father creates a spiritual covering your children will feel even when they can't explain it. Don't underestimate the impact of a whispered prayer or a tearful plea before God. It's not weakness—it's spiritual warfare, and it changes things.

Reflect
- How can I become more intentional and consistent in praying for my children?
- What specific areas of my children's lives should I begin lifting up to God today?

Prayer Moment
Father,
Thank You for the privilege of lifting my children before You. I may not always know what they need, but You do. Teach me to be faithful in prayer —to pray not just when things are hard, but every day.

Cover their hearts with Your protection, guide their steps in Your truth, and draw them close to You all their days. Help me to believe that my prayers are powerful because You are powerful. Let my legacy be one of faith-filled intercession, and let my children see Your hand in their lives through every answered prayer.

In Jesus' name,
Amen.

Day 27
Trusting God with Their Future

Scripture:

"Trust in the Lord with all your heart and lean not on your own understanding; in all your ways submit to Him, and He will make your paths straight."
— Proverbs 3:5–6 (NIV)

Devotion

As a father, one of the hardest things to do is to release control and trust God with your children's future. You want to protect them, guide them, and ensure they make the right decisions. But the truth is, no matter how involved you are, there are places only God can lead them.

This familiar passage in Proverbs is not just for your children—it's for you. God calls you to trust Him fully, even when you don't understand what's happening in their lives. That means surrendering your fears, your plans, and your timing.

When you trust God with their future, you're showing your children what faith looks like. You're teaching them to rely on God by modeling a heart that leans on Him. Your peace in uncertain times becomes a steady voice in their minds when they face their own storms.

You are not letting go—you are placing them in the safest hands possible. And in doing so, you're building a legacy that says, "Our hope is not in ourselves—it is in the Lord."

Reflect
- What fears or concerns about my children's future do I need to surrender to God today?
- How can I demonstrate trust in God in a way that strengthens my children's own faith?

Prayer Moment
God,
You love my children more than I ever could, and You see their future from beginning to end. Help me to surrender my need for control and choose faith over fear. Teach me to trust You not only with my life but with theirs.

When I'm tempted to worry, remind me of Your promises. Give me peace as I release them into Your care, and courage to guide them without clinging to them. May my trust in You lead them to trust You too.

In Jesus' name,
Amen.

Day 28
Enduring Faith

Scripture:
"Therefore, since we are surrounded by such a great cloud of witnesses, let us throw off everything that hinders and the sin that so easily entangles. And let us run with perseverance the race marked out for us, fixing our eyes on Jesus, the pioneer and perfecter of faith."
— Hebrews 12:1–2 (NIV)

Devotion
Faith isn't just about how you start—it's about how you finish. As a father, you are running a race that your children are watching closely. They're learning what perseverance looks like, not in your perfection, but in your refusal to quit when things get hard.

The legacy of faith you leave isn't shaped by mountaintop moments alone; it's built in the valleys, in the ordinary days, and in the decisions to press on when you feel weak. Hebrews 12 calls us to throw off distractions and keep our eyes on Jesus. Why? Because He ran before us—and He empowers us to finish well.

Enduring faith doesn't mean you'll never stumble. It means that even when you do, you get back up, fix your eyes on Jesus, and keep going. That's what your children need to see—a father who perseveres, who trusts, and who continues to walk with God even through storms.

You are running for more than yourself. The race you finish well becomes a path your children can follow with confidence.

Reflect
- What areas in my life are hindering me from running my race with endurance?
- How can I daily fix my eyes on Jesus in a way that my children will remember?

Prayer Moment
Lord,

Give me the strength to run this race with endurance. Help me to shake off the things that weigh me down—worry, distraction, sin—and keep my eyes on You. I want to leave behind a legacy of faith that shows my children how to persevere.

Even when I'm tired, remind me that You are with me. Help me to be faithful in the small things, consistent in prayer, and committed to walking with You daily. Let my life speak of Your grace, Your power, and Your faithfulness to the end.

In Jesus' name,
Amen.

MY NOTES & PRAYERS

Day 29
Leaving a Spiritual Legacy

Scripture:
"I am reminded of your sincere faith, which first lived in your grandmother Lois and in your mother Eunice and, I am persuaded, now lives in you also."
— 2 Timothy 1:5 (NIV)

Devotion
A spiritual legacy is not built overnight—it's cultivated through years of faithfulness, intentionality, and love. Paul commended Timothy's sincere faith, passed down from his grandmother and mother. Though not a fatherly example in this verse, it paints a powerful picture: faith can be inherited—not just biologically, but spiritually.

As a father, you are laying down spiritual footprints that your children will either follow or question. Your prayers, your time in the Word, the way you handle adversity, the grace you offer, and the consistency of your character —these are the seeds that grow into legacy.

Legacy isn't just about what people remember you for—it's about what you pass on that outlives you. You may never fully see the results in your lifetime, but a sincere faith planted today can bless generations after you're gone.

You don't need to be perfect—you need to be present, intentional, and faithful. By living out your faith daily, you are giving your children something far greater than wealth or worldly success: you are giving them a foundation to build their own relationship with God.

Reflect

- What parts of my faith do I most want to pass down to my children?
- In what ways can I be more intentional about creating a spiritual legacy today?

Prayer Moment

Father,

Thank You for entrusting me with the gift of fatherhood. Help me to live a life that inspires and encourages lasting faith in my children. Let my walk with You be genuine and consistent, a reflection of Your grace and truth.

Teach me to speak life, to pray with purpose, and to model humility and strength. May my children inherit not just my name, but a clear and unwavering testimony of Your goodness. Let the legacy I leave be rooted in You and bear fruit in their lives for generations to come.

In Jesus' name,
Amen.

Day 30
Well Done, Father

Scripture:

"His master replied, 'Well done, good and faithful servant! You have been faithful with a few things; I will put you in charge of many things. Come and share your master's happiness!'"
— Matthew 25:21 (NIV)

Devotion

One day, every earthly role—including the sacred calling of fatherhood—will come to an end. What will remain is the eternal impact of how faithfully we walked with God and led our families. In Matthew 25, Jesus speaks of the servant who was faithful with what he was given. He wasn't praised for being flawless, famous, or strong—he was honored for being faithful.

Fathers, your reward is not found in how impressive you appear, but in how faithfully you serve. God sees the quiet sacrifices, the whispered prayers, the daily disciplines, and the love that often goes unnoticed. He sees when you stay the course even when it's hard. And He will say, "Well done."

You may wonder if you're doing enough, being enough, leading well enough. Take heart—God doesn't require perfection. He simply calls you to trust Him, follow Him, and keep showing up. If you've done that, you've done well.

Let your legacy not just be about what you've built—but who you've become: a father who finished his race with faith, love, and integrity.

Reflect
- If today were the final chapter of your story, what would you want your children to remember most about your faith?
- What does "finishing well" look like for you in this season of fatherhood?

Prayer Moment
Father,
Thank You for the journey You've led me on through fatherhood. I know I haven't always gotten it right, but You've been faithful. Help me to finish well—to keep leading my family with courage, humility, and deep trust in You.

I long to hear You say, "Well done." Give me strength for each step ahead, grace for my shortcomings, and joy in the seeds I've sown. May my life reflect Your love and truth, and may my children grow up knowing the reality of Your presence because of what they saw in me.

In Jesus' name,
Amen.

Weekly Check-in

What are three things I'm grateful for this week?

1. ....

2. ....

3. ....

What am I praying for this week?

....

....

....

....

....

How did I reflect God's Love this week?

....

....

....

....

....

What areas of my life do I need to improve / surrender to Christ so that I may be more like Him?

....

....

....

....

....

"You can't pour from an empty cup—take care of yourself first."

Faith that Pleases God

Scripture:
"And without faith it is impossible to please God, because anyone who comes to him must believe that he exists and that he rewards those who earnestly seek him."
— Hebrews 11:6 (NIV)

Devotion
As a father, you want to provide for your family, protect them, and lead them well. But above all, God is calling you to be a man of faith—because faith is what pleases Him most.

Faith isn't just believing that God exists—it's living like He's with you, for you, and working through you. It's trusting Him when things are uncertain. It's obeying Him even when the outcome isn't guaranteed. And it's seeking Him daily—not just for what He can give, but because He alone is worth pursuing.

Your children may not remember every lesson you teach, but they will remember the way you live. A father who walks by faith models a life that says, "God is real, God is good, and God is trustworthy."

Let your home be shaped by a faith that seeks God—not just in crisis, but in quiet moments, daily decisions, and long seasons of waiting. That kind of faith plants deep roots and leaves a lasting legacy.

Reflect

- Am I seeking God with a heart that desires relationship—or just relief?
- How can I demonstrate to my family that faith is not just belief, but a daily pursuit of God?

Prayer Moment

God,

Thank You that faith is what moves Your heart—not perfection or performance. Help me to live with the kind of faith that pleases You. Make me a man who seeks You earnestly—not just when I need something, but because I desire to walk closely with You.

Teach me to trust You in the unknown, to obey even when it's hard, and to believe that You are always at work for my good and Your glory. Let my faith be an anchor for my family—strong, steady, and visible.

Fill my heart with hunger for Your presence. Let my life reflect a deep and growing faith that my children can follow.

In Jesus' name,
Amen.

The Foundation of a Father's Faith

Scripture:
"But as for me and my household, we will serve the Lord." — Joshua 24:15 (NIV)

Devotion

Every home is built on something—ambition, tradition, culture. But for a father of faith, the home is built on a deeper foundation: a relationship with God. Joshua made a bold and clear declaration that still echoes through generations—"As for me and my household, we will serve the Lord." It was more than a personal decision; it was a leadership choice.

As a father, your faith sets the tone. When you prioritize prayer, worship, and Scripture, you're shaping the spiritual atmosphere of your home. You're not just raising children—you're raising disciples, future leaders, and kingdom influencers.

It doesn't mean being perfect. It means being authentic. Let your children see you seek God, depend on Him, and walk with Him even in struggles. Faith isn't just taught—it's caught.

Reflect

- What is currently shaping the spiritual foundation of my home?
- How can I lead my family more intentionally toward serving the Lord?

Prayer Moment

Lord,

Thank You for the sacred calling to lead my family in faith. I don't take this responsibility lightly—it is both a great honor and a great challenge. Teach me daily how to shepherd my home with wisdom, compassion, and unwavering commitment to Your truth.

Help me to build our family's foundation on Your Word—not just in words, but in the way I live, love, and lead. May every decision, every conversation, and every act of service reflect the values of Your kingdom. Let my life be a steady example of trust in You, especially in times of uncertainty or hardship.

Give me the boldness to declare, like Joshua, "As for me and my house, we will serve the Lord." Let that not just be a declaration on our walls, but a truth etched in our hearts. Strengthen my leadership with humility, cover my weaknesses with Your grace, and let Your presence guide every step we take as a family.

In Jesus' name,
Amen.

Strength in Surrender

Scripture:

"Trust in the Lord with all your heart and lean not on your own understanding; in all your ways submit to him, and he will make your paths straight." — Proverbs 3:5–6 (NIV)

Devotion

Fatherhood often demands answers, strength, and direction. But the truth is—there will be days when you don't know what to do. That's okay. God never asked you to be all-knowing—He asks you to trust Him.

Surrender is not weakness; it's the deepest form of strength. When you acknowledge your limits and lean on God's wisdom, you're not only growing as a man of faith, but also teaching your children that real strength begins with humility.

When they see you praying through confusion, seeking God's will in decisions, and trusting Him even when life feels uncertain, they learn that faith is more than words—it's a daily dependence on a faithful God.

God honors your surrender. He doesn't expect perfection. He expects trust.

Reflect
- What area of my life or fatherhood do I need to surrender to God today?
- How can I model trusting God in front of my children this week?

Prayer Moment
Heavenly Father,
I admit that I don't always have the answers. There are moments when I feel uncertain, overwhelmed, or inadequate in my role as a father. But I thank You that I don't have to have it all figured out—because You do.

Help me to lay down my pride, my fears, and my carefully made plans at Your feet. Teach me to trust You with the unknown, and to find peace not in my control, but in Your perfect sovereignty. Shape my heart to listen for Your voice and respond with obedience.

Lead me with wisdom that goes beyond my understanding and grace that covers my every shortcoming. I want to lead my family not with pressure, but with purpose—not in my own strength, but with confidence in Yours.

Thank You that Your strength is made perfect in my weakness, and that when I lean into You, I will not fall. Remind me daily that You are my source, my guide, and my example. Equip me to be the father You've called me to be.

In Jesus' name,
Amen.

A Father Who Listens

Scripture:
"Everyone should be quick to listen, slow to speak and slow to become angry." — James 1:19 (NIV)

Devotion

One of the greatest gifts you can give your children isn't advice—it's your attention. In a world full of noise, a father who listens is a rare and powerful presence.

Listening is an act of love. It communicates, "You matter. I value you." When you pause to hear your child's thoughts, questions, or even their silence, you're opening a door for trust and connection. And when you listen to them, you're also modeling how to listen to God.

James reminds us to be quick to listen, slow to speak, and slow to anger. That kind of posture doesn't come naturally—it takes intentional faith. But with God's help, you can become the kind of father whose words build up and whose ears are always open.

God, your heavenly Father, always hears you. Let your children know you're listening too.

Reflect

- Have I truly listened to my children lately—not just their words, but their hearts?
- How can I be more intentional about being slow to speak and quick to listen this week?

Prayer Moment

Father,

Thank You for always hearing me—even when my words are clumsy or few. You are never too busy, never distracted, and never distant. Your attentive love teaches me what it means to truly listen.

Lord, teach me to listen more. Quiet the noise around me and within me so I can hear Your still, small voice. Help me to be fully present with my family —to listen not only with my ears, but with my heart. Let me truly hear the unspoken needs of my children and the hopes and burdens of my spouse.

Slow me down when I rush. Soften my words when I'm quick to respond. Give me the grace to speak with kindness and the wisdom to know when silence is more powerful than speech.

May my listening heart reflect Yours—attentive, patient, and full of love. Let my home be a place where every voice is valued and where Your presence is known through peace and understanding.

In Jesus' name,
Amen.

A Father's Legacy

Scripture:

"As a father has compassion on his children, so the Lord has compassion on those who fear him." — Psalm 103:13 (NIV)

Devotion

Being a father is both a divine calling and a daily challenge. You're called to guide, protect, provide, and most importantly—love. Yet with so many responsibilities, it's easy to feel stretched thin or even question if you're doing enough.

But Scripture reminds us that fatherhood mirrors God's own heart. Psalm 103:13 tells us that God, our heavenly Father, is full of compassion. That means being a good father doesn't require perfection—it requires presence. It's not about having all the answers, but about showing up, loving deeply, and leading your family with grace.

Your children won't always remember what you said, but they'll remember how you made them feel—seen, valued, safe. When you pray with them, speak life into them, and model faith and humility, you're laying down a legacy that outlives you.

You don't have to be a perfect dad. Just a present one. And when you fall short (as all do), God's grace is sufficient. Lean on Him daily for the strength to lead your family well.

Reflect

- In what ways can I better reflect God's compassion to my children this week?
- What kind of spiritual legacy am I building for my family?

Prayer Moment

Father God,

Thank You for the incredible honor and sacred responsibility of being a dad. I don't take it lightly that You've entrusted these precious lives into my care. In every season—whether filled with laughter or laced with challenges—remind me that fatherhood is one of the greatest callings You've placed on my life.

Help me to reflect Your heart to my children—not just in what I say, but in how I live. Let them see in me a picture of Your kindness, Your strength, Your mercy, and Your truth. Shape my character so that, in my presence, they can catch a glimpse of Yours.

Give me patience when I am weary—when the days feel long, when the nights feel short, and when my strength is not enough. Fill me with Your Spirit so I respond with gentleness instead of frustration, and grace instead of anger.

Grant me wisdom when I'm unsure of what to say, how to lead, or which path to choose. Remind me that I don't have to do this alone, for You promise to guide those who trust in You. Help me lean into Your Word for direction, and into prayer for peace.

Above all, clothe me with compassion in every moment. Let my children know they are deeply loved—by me and by You. May my words build them up, my actions point them to Jesus, and my love remind them of their identity in You.

Lord, let my life leave behind a legacy—not of perfection, but of faith, love, and grace. A legacy that reaches beyond today and echoes into future generations. One that brings glory to Your name.

In Jesus' name,
Amen.

A Final Word of Encouragement

You've completed Fatherhood & Faith: A 30-Day Devotional for Dads. But this is not the end—it's a new beginning.

Every prayer you've prayed, every truth you've meditated on, and every step you've taken toward Christ has laid a foundation for lasting impact. Your willingness to grow spiritually will not only shape your life but will echo through the generations that follow.

As you continue this journey, remember:

- You are not alone—God is with you.
- You don't need to be perfect—just present and faithful.
- Your legacy is not built in a day—it's built daily.

Keep seeking Him. Keep leading with love. Keep trusting God with your family, your future, and your fatherhood.

ABOUT THE AUTHOR

Daniel Okumbele is a devoted husband, father, and passionate follower of Christ. With a heart for encouraging men in their walk with God, he writes with honesty, humility, and a deep commitment to biblical truth. Drawing from real-life experience and years of ministry, Daniel helps fathers embrace their God-given role with courage, grace, and faith.

Through his devotionals, mentoring, and teaching, Daniel equips dads to lead their families with love and integrity while deepening their own relationship with God. He believes that when a father walks in faith, generations are changed.

When he's not writing, you'll find him spending time with his family, serving in his local church, and enjoying the simple, sacred moments of everyday life.

"The righteous man walks in his integrity; his children are blessed after him."
—Proverbs 20:7

A Father's Blessing:

May God strengthen your hands, soften your heart, and fill your home with peace.
May your children rise and call you blessed, and may your life reflect the love of the Perfect Father—our God and King.
In all you do, may you walk in faith, lead with grace,
and leave a legacy rooted in Christ.
Amen.